LEARN2LEAD

Learn2Lead
© FIEC / The Good Book Company Ltd, 2007

The Good Book Company
Elm House, 37 Elm Road, New Malden, Surrey KT3 3HB, UK
Tel: 0845-225-0880
Fax: 0845-225-0990
Email: admin@thegoodbook.co.uk
Internet: www.thegoodbook.co.uk

ISBN 13: 978 1905564736

Printed in India

LEARN2LEAD

LEADERSHIP IN PRACTICE 1

WELCOME

Welcome to the *Leadership in Practice 1* track of the *Learn2Lead* course – part of the local-church leadership training programme initially developed by the Fellowship of Independent Evangelical Churches. We hope you find this course both enjoyable and useful to your life and ministry.

It is likely that you will be using this book as part of a group within your congregation. But it is also possible to work through this material alone. Whichever method applies to you, we would encourage you to work prayerfully and diligently through the material, taking every opportunity to discuss the work with Christians around you.

CONTENTS

LEADERSHIP IN PRACTICE 1

	PREFACE	6
4.1	USING THE BIBLE	11
4.2	HITTING THE TARGET	16
4.3	CARING FOR INDIVIDUALS	22
4.4	BUILDING THE TEAM	26
4.5	LEADING A HOME GROUP	30
4.6	LEADING GOD'S PEOPLE IN WORSHIP	36
4.7	LEADING GOD'S PEOPLE IN PRAYER	42
4.8	PLANNING AND PREPARING	47
4.9	DEVELOPING A STRATEGY	50
4.10	IMPLEMENTING THE STRATEGY	55

PREFACE

'THE THINGS YOU HAVE HEARD me say in the presence of many witnesses entrust to reliable men who will also be qualified to teach others' (2 Timothy 2:2)

Developing leaders in the church is the purpose of *Learn2Lead*. Leadership of the body of Christ is important, and therefore taking time to develop the leaders of the future is a vital aspect of building up God's church.

LEADERSHIP IS THE KEY

If you asked your Christian friends to sum up their feelings about contemporary church life, two of the words that would crop up most frequently might well be *frustration* and *disappointment*. How can that be? It's not because there's anything wrong with the gospel. That is still the power of God for the salvation of everyone who believes in the Lord Jesus Christ. It may be something to do with the way we do church. God has given us all the resources we need to fulfil his plans for this generation, but there is a crying need to discover, nurture, train and liberate the ministries of people within the church. And that means competent and effective leadership.

CHANGING THE CULTURE

Many of us come from a background where everyone expected the Minister to do everything – except perhaps play the organ, teach Sunday School or make the tea. And more disturbingly, the Minister expected it to be that way too. The vision for *Learn2Lead* is to create a culture where everyone in the church – especially young people – see leadership as something they aspire to. When Paul wrote to Timothy, he obviously expected that there would be people in the church who wanted to be leaders. We want people in the church to see their leaders at work and say, 'Under God, I'd love to be able to do that!'

WHAT IS LEARN2LEAD?

Learn2Lead is an introductory course for church members who are not in a position to take time off work for more preparation for their role as leaders. It draws on the experience of the team that already trains people through a residential and placement programme called *Prepared for Service*. When you have completed *Learn2Lead* you may consider further study under the *Prepared for Service* programme or alternatively, with the Open Bible Institute. Details of these organisations can be found at the end of this workbook.

WHO TEACHES LEARN2LEAD?

The Scriptures indicate that those who are already doing important work in the church have it as their responsibility to train others to carry forward the work. The apostle Paul told his son in the faith, Timothy, 'The things you have heard me say in the presence of many witnesses entrust to reliable men who will also be qualified to teach others' (2 Timothy 2:2).

Learn2Lead is a tool for experienced leaders to use to teach others. It is designed to help those 'at the helm' to assist a new generation of leaders as they learn how to lead others. Tutors will normally be church leaders and others whose ministry has earned the respect and confidence of those they lead.

WHO MARKS LEARN2LEAD?

Learn2Lead is a course designed for use within your congregation under the guidance of your church leader. Their feedback is going to be the most beneficial to you as they know you as a person and see your ministry in action. However, you may also like an independent person to look at your work, mark it and (if successful) issue you with a certificate that acknowledges your many hours of study. If this is the case then you are welcome to submit a folder of your work (containing answers to each of the exercises in this book) to the Open Bible Institute. For full details (including the current marking fee) please see the website: *www.open-bible-institute.org*.

WHO IS LEARN2LEAD FOR?

It is for everyone in the local church who has the potential to be a leader. And the definition of leadership? That quality that makes other people want to follow you. You may be in leadership already as an elder or youth work co-ordinator. Perhaps people in the church have suggested that you have the leadership gifts that could be developed for the future. *Learn2Lead* is not just for potential church leaders, it is also hoped that it will assist any church member who is given responsibility in the church.

FIVE TRACKS

Learn2Lead consists of five tracks of training looking at the knowledge, skills and attitudes required to be developed by leaders in the church.

Understanding the Bible, Understanding Doctrine, Understanding Leadership, Leadership in Practice 1 and Leadership in Practice 2

THREE ELEMENTS TO THE COURSE

There are three elements to the course:

1. **Individual study** – this should be done before meeting with your tutor and the group.
2. **Group session** – this would normally include a review of individual study; discussion of some of the answers; review of any action points from the previous group session and preview of the next unit to be studied etc.
3. **Ministry opportunity** – there may be ways in which the study material from the unit can be implemented in your own ministry.

So *Learn2Lead* is not just about gathering information and getting the answers right but also applying that information so that you learn by experience in the church.

THE TOOLS YOU WILL NEED

- **Bible** – *Learn2Lead* uses the NIV Bible throughout.

- **Notebook** – You will need to make a record of your answers to questions and other notes and we suggest you have a notebook which you can use in conjunction with this student manual. At the end of these ten units, there is the option to submit the work you have done for marking by the Open Bible Institute. All students who submit work of an appropriate standard will be issued with a certificate. If you would like to work towards this certificate, please keep all your answers to the unit questions in your notebook. Once you have finished unit 10, neat versions of your answers can be submitted to the Open Bible Institute with the appropriate marking fee.

- **Bible Dictionary** – It would be useful for you to have access to a good Bible Dictionary. Student discounts are available through the Open Bible Institute office.

• The Bible passages by this symbol must be read. There are also a number of other references which should be looked at if you have time.

• These questions are designed to be worked through on your own and usually have factual answers.

• These questions are designed for discussion during your group meeting. Come prepared with some ideas.

• The six Old Testament units from Understanding the Bible have questions with this symbol. They are important as they show the 'big picture' of what God planned and did through Jesus Christ throughout history.

• These are points of application and further work which will help you to develop what you have learned in the unit.

The value of *Learn2Lead* is not only found in the quality of the material but particularly in its application. This is the secret of effective leadership in the body of Christ. The *Learn2Lead* team are interested in ensuring that the words contained within this book come alive in your role of leadership and in the church as a whole. If you can help us develop the material to ensure that this continues to happen please contact us, we would love to hear how you are progressing.

Remember leadership is action – never just a position!

Learn2Lead c/o The Good Book Company,
Elm House, 37 Elm Road, New Malden, Surrey KT3 3HB
For further information please also see the FIEC website: www.fiec.org.uk

USING THE BIBLE

MANY LEADERSHIP qualities apply equally both to Christians and non-Christians. However, a defining quality in every Christian leader is a firm grasp of the word of God. The aim of this Unit is to show the importance of the Bible for Christian leadership and how to use it. 'You can't believe the Bible – it's full of contradictions'. 'You can use the Bible to prove anything'. 'It's all a matter of interpretation.' Comments like these may undermine our confidence in the Bible. In fact, God has interpreted the gospel for us in the Bible.

Read 1 Corinthians 15:3

Identify three things from that verse which are essential to the Christian's faith...
- *The fact – what happened*
- *The source – how we know*
- *The explanation – what it means to us*

GET INTO THE BIBLE

 Read Joshua 1:1-10

What components might make up an army officer's training course at Sandhurst? Military History? Knowing Your Enemy? Advanced Military Strategy? ... these would all certainly be included. Joshua needs all these skills as he leads the Israelites into the promised land. Picture the scene in Joshua's tent as the General gathers his commanders for their final briefing. There are maps and charts everywhere. And, of course, the strategy for taking Jericho is a little out of the ordinary and will take some explaining. What does Joshua do? He remembers the word of the Lord and says, 'Now before we go any further, let's read the Scriptures'. If a busy general before a crucial battle needs to draw on his Bible, so do those of us involved in leadership in the church today.

WHY IS THE BIBLE VITAL FOR LEADERSHIP?

Match the reasons given on the left to the Scriptures quoted on the right in the diagram below.

The Bible is a vital weapon in our spiritual warfare and we need to know how to use it	John 5:39
God has given us the Scriptures so that we may be thoroughly equipped for every task he has in mind for us	Ephesians 5:25-26
The word of God has a direct bearing upon our purity of heart and mind as believers	Ephesians 6:17
The Bible reveals Jesus to us, who is our supreme leader	2 Timothy 3:16-17
The Bible is our supreme source of guidance through life	Psalm 119:105

You cannot expect to be an effective spiritual leader if you do not make the Bible a priority in your life.

HOW TO INTERPRET THE BIBLE

Read Titus 1:1-5

Ask yourself these questions:
- *Who is the writer?*
- *To whom is he writing and when?*
- *Why is he writing?*
- *What is the main purpose of his letter?*

There are three steps to studying the Scriptures:
1. *Context – Why is this passage here? How does it fit into Scripture? How does it fit into the book to which it belongs?*
2. *Content – What is its main theme or point? Who are its main characters? What is happening? Identify the key words.*
3. *Consequences – What will be the outcomes of our study? They could be many and various, personal and/or communal, and related to belief and/or behaviour.*

Take the time to learn the rules of interpretation well. If we fail at this point, we will go astray ourselves and run the risk of leading others with us. At the very least, we risk denying them an understanding of all that God has provided for us in Christ.

THE RULES OF INTERPRETATION

1. **The grammar** – Scripture has only one meaning. So·
   - What kind of literature is it? Laws are very different from proverbs. Look back over Track 1, Understanding the Bible: *Setting the scene – the Bible as literature.*
   - Take the text at face value unless there is good reason for not doing so – such as, for example, when dealing with a poem or a parable.
   - What do the individual words mean? John uses the word 'world' in his Gospel several times. What does he mean by it?
   - Is there a natural structure or flow to the passage? Is there a key question or a punch-line that sets the agenda?
   - Watch out for figurative language like, 'I am the true vine'.
   - When interpreting parables, don't try to analyse every detail, but go for the big idea.
2. The **history and the geography** – when do the events described take place, and where? Remember the Bible has an unfolding storyline which is why the Understanding the Bible Track of *Learn2Lead* is so useful.

• Read your study passage in the light of biblical history. Why is the birth of Cain such a big event in Genesis 4? And such a big disappointment? For the answer, review God's response to the Fall in Genesis 3.

• Names, places or events often carry symbolic meanings. Look for the clues in the text itself.

3. **The theology** – what does this passage mean in the unfolding message of the gospel?

• How does it fit into the book? Into its Testament? Into the whole Bible?

• How does it relate to other parts of Scripture? Because it is God's word, Scripture cannot contradict Scripture. So, if you're not sure what your passage means, find a parallel and see if that helps to unlock the meaning.

We all have our presuppositions as we approach a passage. As you become more familiar with the Bible, allow it to mould your mental framework so that your presuppositions themselves become truly biblical.

Now, gather your background material together and start to ask some of the basic Bible questions:

• What did this passage say to its original hearers? What did it tell them about God? About the world they lived in? About his plans for them?

• What does this passage have to say to us? And what do we need to do about it?

Using this approach, think of some of the different ways you could study the Bible.

Take a look at Titus 2:11-14

Prepare a five-minute outline, showing how this doctrinal passage serves Paul's practical purpose in the whole letter.

THE IMPORTANCE OF PREPARATION

It's an appealing thought that God will inspire us with the necessary words on the spur of the moment. And sometimes he does! But don't imagine that he blesses laziness.

What do these passages teach about the importance of prayerful preparation?
- *2 Timothy 2:15*
- *2 Timothy 3:14-17*
- *Ecclesiastes 12:9-12*

REMEMBER YOUR PEOPLE

Read Colossians 1:28-29

Paul was a purpose-driven man. We need to follow his example. The Bible was not given to increase our knowledge but to change our lives. In leadership, you will need to keep your people in mind all the time.
- Remember their needs, their sins, their hopes and fears
- God has given you the Bible as the great instrument for change in their lives.

THINK IT THROUGH

Our critics sometimes claim that we worship the Bible. The language of some of the psalms comes pretty close to it at times. Take Psalm 119:48 for example:
Is the psalmist guilty?
What is he saying?
Why does he feel so strongly about the Bible?
What about you?

FOLLOW IT UP

Take a Bible passage which you will be using in your ministry (for a talk, Bible study or lesson) and follow the rules of interpretation. How have those rules helped you to use the Bible more effectively?

HITTING THE TARGET

LOOK BACK at Unit 3.7 in *Understanding Leadership: Dealing with People*. There is reference there to the three-fold responsibilities of leaders: the achievement of tasks, the management of teams and the care of individuals. This Unit and the next two will help you to identify how you can satisfy the requirements of the task (this Unit), the needs of the individual (*Caring for individuals*) and the effectiveness of the team (*Building the team*).

SETTING TARGETS

Everyone sets targets these days. The rail companies must run 95% of their trains on time, 999 calls must be responded to within so many minutes, hospital waiting lists must be reduced to a certain level. Yet often in church we have been slow to set targets or to establish priorities for our ministry.

1. Is it right to set targets?
2. What are the benefits and dangers we face when we do so?

SETTING PERSONAL PRIORITIES

Read Matthew 28:16-20

The Great Commission is a key New Testament passage. Here the risen Lord Jesus sets the agenda for his church from the time of Pentecost right through to Judgement Day and the end of the world.

Think about the following questions:
1. What is the ultimate target of the church in this passage?
2. How, according to Jesus here, is this target to be achieved?

One American President put a sign on his desk in the Oval Office saying, 'It's the economy, stupid!' In a graphic way, he wanted to remind himself that the success or failure of his presidency lay in the health of the American economy. That would be his bottom line.

If you were to capture the target of the church in a one-liner on your desk, what would it be?

Read Philippians 3:7-11

Paul has a lot of things on his mind at this point in his ministry. Scan the letter so far and make a list of the things that might be concerning him just now. Then, coming back to the above five verses, what one thing occupies him above all others?

Your own personal walk with God must always be your number one target. Everything you do rises or falls with this. Jesus says, *'Apart from me you can do nothing!'* (John 15:5)

TARGETS FOR MY MINISTRY

The old maxim is right, 'If you aim at nothing, you're sure to hit it!' Learn to target your effort.

If you were to capture the target of your ministry in a one-liner, what would it be?

Qualify it with the following checks.

1. Be clear about the focus of your ministry. Don't be afraid to ask the hard questions like:
   • How many people have been affected by this ministry in the last year?
   • What does it cost in time and money to fulfil this ministry?
   • Would it need to be replaced with something else if we shut it down?
   • If we didn't do this, what else could we do?
2. Set targets that can be achieved with a bit of effort.
3. Set targets that lie within your ability; eg revival in your Sunday School may be a brilliant dream, but it's not in your power to pull it off.
4. Set targets that fulfil the demands of the Great Commission. Remember, church is all about making disciples; your ministry must be too.
5. Build into your targets issues like how you are going to achieve them, and when.
6. Set targets that you can measure in, say, six months' time. That way, you can see how you're doing and indulge in a bit of fine-tuning if necessary.
7. Set targets in prayer with others, so that this is not your personal wish-list but a vision given by God and shared and owned by the rest of your team.

Describe some of the symptoms of the disorganised leader.

Think about the life of the Lord Jesus. Every movement is followed … every word monitored … every action analysed… every gesture commented on. He has no private life to speak of. Yet he never seems to hurry. Not only does he manage his public appointments perfectly without a secretary, but he also makes time to spend alone with his Heavenly Father. Link the references on the right to the qualities on the left in the chart below.

He understands his mission	Luke 9:1-10
He understands his limits	Luke 18:31-19:10
He understands his disciples	Luke 22:39-46

How can we apply these lessons to ourselves?
- *know yourself – how do you best tick? How much sleep do you need? Do you work better early in the morning or late at night? Are you getting enough exercise?*
- *know your priorities – seize control of your diary, and budget time for the things that are vital to your ministries at home and at church*
- *plan long-term – it's better to put the important things first before dealing with secondary priorities rather than the other way round.*

THINK IT THROUGH

Go back to the Great Commission. Think through the various activities which take place in your church, like...
- *the Sunday services*
- *the way you do young people's work*
- *the way you invest your money*
- *the way you structure your building*

To what extent are these activities governed by the goal set for us by the Lord Jesus?

MAKING DECISIONS

In order to hit the targets of the church or of your ministry decisions have to be made.

Read Acts 6:1-7

Here is the early church reaching a decision. How do the following factors interact:
- *unity*
- *authority*
- *flexibility*
- *priority*

GUIDELINES FOR MAKING DECISIONS

Read the following passages:
- Psalm 133
- Isaiah 57:15
- Matthew 5:3–10
- Acts 13:1–3
- Acts 15:28
- Galatians 5:22–23
- 2 Timothy 3:16–17
- James 1:5

Create a set of guidelines for making decisions.

DIFFERENT TYPES AND LEVELS OF DECISION

Study the youth worker's draft agenda (below). Most items require a decision. Try to identify the different types of decision needed.

LOVEMORE Evangelical Church

Youth Work Action Group • 12 September 2007 – 8:00pm

1. Devotions
2. Minutes of last meeting
3. Matters arising
4. Funding for a full-time youth worker
5. Taking the youth group to Contagious next summer
6. Joining the Lovemore Council of Churches Youth Forum
7. The dismissal of Adam from the Lovemore Drop-in Centre
8. Spring cleaning the youth lounge at church
9. Date of the next meeting

PREPARING FOR A DECISION

With such a wide range of types of decision to be made in church life, the amount of care and preparation varies widely too. A church does not need to enter a period of fasting and prayer if the decision concerns whether to hold the mid-week Bible Study at 7.45 or 8.00pm. It may well feel the need to do so if a serious case of church discipline emerges. The more serious the issue, the greater the care that must be taken.

So, imagine you have someone in mind for a full-time youth worker's post at Lovemore. Consider the steps in the chart overleaf and put them in some kind of order to enable you to reach a decision you can be confident in.

THE ATMOSPHERE FOR DECISIONMAKING

Decisions should always be made in an atmosphere of worship and dependence upon God. Everyone involved should always speak and interact in love, and everything should be done to maintain unity (Psalm 133).They should always trust the motives underlying church decisions (1 Corinthians 10:31-32). Our motives must be:
- the glory of God
- the spread of the gospel
- the good of God's people.

Step	Reason	Order
Gather information	Sound decisions demand the best information we can find. Where appropriate, list the pros and cons in two columns and compare them.	
Discuss	Talk the issues through thoroughly with the people concerned. One reason some church meetings fall into disarray is that matters that are of no interest to the majority are discussed at length with everybody. On the other hand, matters should not be decided until all those concerned have been consulted.	
Read the Bible	What does God say in his word? Study any relevant Bible passages together.	
Defer	If the way forward is not clear or a number of people are not convinced, it may be wise to defer a decision for further discussion, more prayer and additional information. If it is genuinely not possible to defer a decision, explain why. Then commit the matter to the Lord and trust that his sovereign wisdom will overrule.	
Decide	Once all the relevant facts have been gathered, and the issues debated, then a decision should be made.	
Pray	Where the whole church is involved the whole church should pray. Where the elders must decide, they should pray and the church should pray for them, if it is a public matter.	

THINK IT THROUGH

1. *What steps might you take as a leader to sweeten the atmosphere of a meeting when decisions need to be made?*
2. *What steps can you take to keep the unity of the Spirit in the bond of peace?*
3. *Why is democracy a poor model for decision-making in church?*

FOLLOW IT UP

1. *Are there any decisions that must be made by you? How will you go about making them?*
2. *How would you make sure you hit targets in the future? How would you review targets that have been made for your ministry?*

CARING FOR INDIVIDUALS

THE AIM of this unit is to get you thinking about the responsibility God lays upon each of us to care for one another. It is not intended to be a course on counselling which would require specialist training.

FOR STARTERS

Sue is an attractive 36-year-old who is married to Jim, the nicest man you could imagine. They're both Christians actively involved in your church. But Sue is bored. Somehow their marriage is dying on the inside. She knows what God says about divorce but how can he expect her to endure a relationship that demands everything and gives nothing in return? To make matters worse, Sue's boss is a sensitive man who enjoys her company. Occasionally he takes her out to lunch. They talk and laugh and Sue feels alive. In her honest moments, she asks herself if she is being drawn into an affair.

 Somehow, in a casual conversation after church, just a little of how Sue is feeling slips out. What do you do?

Adam is a very dedicated youth leader who devotes long hours to planning the programme, and relating to the children. He is also under time pressures at work. The atmosphere at the club is deteriorating and last week he dealt in a heavy-handed way with a girl who was swearing. When Ruth, who relates very well to the girls, spoke to him about her concerns he became very prickly and she has now said that she doesn't feel the club is honouring God, and that she cannot work with Adam any longer and wants to resign.

1. Ruth and Adam have both spoken to you about this situation. What would you do?

2. To what extent does God intend the church to be a healing community? And you to be part of it?

GET INTO THE BIBLE

Read Hebrews 10:24-25

The author was writing to Christians who were struggling and being tempted to give up. He tells them to hold on (v23) and not throw away their confidence in God (v35). All Christians should be involved in encouragement.

What three commands does he give us in 10:24-25?

Make a list of three ways in which you could spur on a Christian with whom you are working to love and good deeds.

In verse 25 the writer uses the word 'encourage' – a translation of the Greek word *parakaleo*. This is the word Jesus used to describe the Holy Spirit (John 14:16; 15:26). It can be translated 'Counsellor' or 'Comforter'. It is tough to follow the Lord. The ministry of encouragement has been defined as 'helping someone to want to try to be a better Christian even when they feel like giving up'.

How do the following Scriptures help us in this ministry?
- *Romans 12:9-13*
- *Galatians 6:2*
- *Ecclesiastes 4:9-12*

Read Romans 15:14

You would almost be forgiven for thinking that counselling is a 21st century discovery. Not so! Here in this verse we find the Apostle Paul congratulating the Roman Christians on being well able to care for one another without much help from him. The Greek word he uses here is *noutheteo*. Literally, it means to *put in mind* – especially to put someone else in mind of his or her duty – to let them know what they should be doing in a given situation. It's all about encouraging a brother or sister to take a particular course of action or warning them against taking a different course of action! This word *noutheteo* involves counselling… correcting… instructing. The NIV most often renders the word –*to warn!*

WHO DOES IT?

Look again at Romans 15:14

1. Who is to do it?
2. On what basis does Paul make this judgement?

A LOVING HEART

The Roman Christians aren't perfect. We don't need to look far to see that there are tensions in the church.

But what does Paul see in them? And how does this answer an apparent contradiction with what he says in 14:13?

A WISE HEAD

These folk have a good grasp of the Scriptures and how to use them.

Why is that so important? Isn't it all a question of motive (see 2 Timothy 3:16).

The whole purpose of the Scripture is to teach, rebuke, correct and train in righteousness so that the people of God become thoroughly equipped for every good work. The basic tool in all Christian care is the Scripture and before we can contemplate seeking to instruct one another, we must have a good grasp of its teaching ourselves.

HOW ARE WE TO DO IT?

The New Testament is full of examples of instruction and Paul himself is the great model of how it is to be done. Look at these references.
- *Acts 20:31*
- *1 Thessalonians 2:11-12*
- *1 Corinthians 4:14-15*
- *Colossians 4:7-9*

What do you learn from these passages about caring for individuals?

THE DYNAMICS OF CARING

The two double circles in the diagram on page 25 represent you as the leader and the individual for whom you are caring. Inside the inner circle is the heart of each person. You would want to speak heart-to-heart but the outside circles are barriers to this.

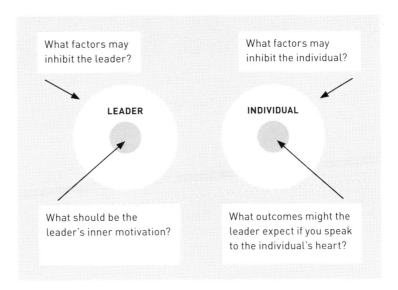

 Study the diagram and answer the questions with reference to the two case studies described on page 22.

COULD I DO IT?

It is obviously Paul's desire that we should be good at helping one another. Perhaps in many churches it has always been left to the Pastor or elders.

 If more are to be involved, write some do's and don'ts to guide them in caring for individuals.

THINK IT THROUGH

 Leaders should be interested in the growth and development of each person for whom they are responsible. Generally this means that leaders should be looking for change in the individual.

Work at a theology of change under these headings:
- the goal of change – what is God looking for?
- the power for change – who facilitates change in the Christian life?
- what can be changed? And what can't? We're all said to be victims these days. How do you deal with those who say that they are victims of their past?
- the process of change – work through the two-factored approach to change which Paul uses in Ephesians 4:17-32.

BUILDING THE TEAM

LOOK BACK at Unit 3:6 of *Understanding Leadership: Working with Teams*. This Unit will help you to identify how to build an effective team of God's people. God's people, the family of believers, the community of faith – these are all phrases used to describe the church. As leaders we have a responsibility to ensure that fellowship is encouraged and that the body of Christ does not become disjointed. In many local churches there are several distinct teams needing to be built together – the elders, the youth workers, home group leaders, the finance team.

Think back to your own experiences of working in a team. Describe the characteristics of the best and worst teams of which you have ever been a part.

Best team	Worst team

GETTING INTO THE BIBLE

Read 1 Corinthians 12

Here is a description of the church as the body of Christ, bringing together a number of different people into the same group. Paul's 'body' analogy helps us as we consider how our teams should work together.

1. Thinking about your role as leader, what does Paul's description mean in the context of the teams with which you are working?

2. What are some important things for a leader to remember when dealing with teams of God's people?

TEAM ROLES

A balanced team should include a diversity of people, all with different roles, but with everyone working together, enabling each other to fulfil the role for which God has equipped them

Can you think of any well-balanced teams:
- *From your experience?*
- *From the Bible?*
- *In your church at the moment?*

Describe them and explain why you think they are 'balanced'.

A leader's responsibility is to develop a well-balanced team with the best possible combination and blend of gifts and skills. One often-quoted team model states that there should be a mix of several different types of people in a team in order for it to work at its best. The different roles needing to be fulfilled in a well-balanced and effective team are described in the panel below. In small teams the members can fulfil more than one role. For example one person could be both an administrator and a coordinator.

1. What do you think is your role in your team?
2. What roles do others fulfil?
3. Are there any roles not mentioned here which are fulfilled by members of your team?
4. Are there any roles which are not being fulfilled? What can you do about it?
5. How can you ensure that each team member accepts the different roles undertaken by others and fulfils his or her own role satisfactorily?

TEAM TASKS

Read Romans 12:1-8

Within this passage Paul describes the members of the church as having different tasks to complete. Make a list of these tasks and record who in your team is fulfilling these in the chart below.

1. Are there any roles which are not mentioned here which are being fulfilled by members of your team?
2. Are any of the mentioned roles not being fulfilled in your team, and what can you do about it?
3. How can you ensure that each team member accepts the different roles of others and fulfils his or her own role satisfactorily?

TEAM ROLE

1. Handling administration; keeping the team's targets in focus.
2. Leading and co-ordinating; ensuring all views are heard and keeping things moving.
3. Driving the task forward.
4. Generating new ideas.
5. Helping the group by using contacts; finding resources.
6. Testing ideas; assessing whether the team is meeting its objectives.
7. Managing conflict and promoting harmony.
8. Pushing the team to meet deadlines; suggesting conclusions.

Role	Team Member

THINK IT THROUGH

Colossians 3:12-17 gives some instruction for teams of God's people working together. What guidelines would you give to members of a new team as they get together for the first time?

FOLLOW IT UP

1. Create an action plan for the team with which you work, implementing the ideas in this Unit.

2. There is a great variety of team roles. The responsibility of the leader in building the team is to help individuals to recognise their gifts and to put them to work in the right role.

- *What gifts do you identify in yourself?*
- *What are the impressions of others with regard to your gifts? You may wish to talk about this with those who are close to you –your present leaders, mentors or advisors.*
- *How will you recognise the gifts of others in your team and help them to put them to work?*

LEADING A HOME GROUP

GET INTO THE BIBLE

Meetings in homes are extremely popular in today's church.

 What are the advantages and disadvantages of Christians meeting in homes as opposed to church buildings?

 Read Acts 2:46, 5:42, 12:12, Romans 16:5, 1 Corinthians 16:19 and Colossians 4:15

 What conclusions do you reach about the way in which homes were used in the early church?

The vast majority of meetings of the New Testament church took place in people's homes. Church buildings proliferated from the 3rd Century AD, but the use of homes has frequently recurred in times of spiritual-awakening. For example, house meetings were widespread during the 18th Century Methodist revival.

GROUP PURPOSE

 1. Brainstorm:
- *some of the advantages of home groups – for church members, leaders and the church's mission.*
- *Are there potential dangers?*
- *Are there Scriptures to back your case?*

2. There are many possible reasons for having home groups – here are just two of them:
- *to pray for each other – your families, work and practical needs*

• to study the Bible together
Can you think of any others?

Your church leaders need to know why the home group exists. Your home group leaders need to know why the home group exists. The home group members need to know why the home group exists. If no one is sure why it exists, the home group will drift. If the church leaders, home group leader, and members have different agendas then the home group will pull apart.

Formulate a purpose statement for your home group beginning, 'Our home group exists to...'

When you know why you have your group you will be able to work out what the leaders' responsibilities are and who else will be needed to share the load. Your quarterly programme and the schedule for each evening will flow out of the purpose statement.

WANTED – HOME GROUP LEADER

The church leaders will appoint home group leaders and in an ideal church they will know what they want them to do.

Attempt a job description – a list of responsibilities to fulfil – for the home group leader(s) in your church, bearing in mind the purpose of home groups.

A SENSE OF BELONGING

1. How can the leader help the home group members to feel a sense of ownership – that 'this is my group'?

2. What level of commitment is it reasonable to expect of the members of your group. A typical group may include, for example, a high-flying (in both senses) executive, a single mum with young children, a couple in their 70s, a single teacher, a manual worker paying off debts and the Friday night youth club leader.

THE HOME GROUP MEETING

1. Place – what criteria should you bear in mind when choosing a home in which to meet?

2. Time – how do you decide on an appropriate start and finish time for your group? How rigid should you be? When the home group meets, what balance should there be between formal content and informal fellowship?

3. Comment on the following accounts of such group meetings:

From a leader:

'We had a wonderful time in our group last night in our Bible study on Noah, partly perhaps because Angela couldn't come. She does talk a lot about herself, even though we are really there to hear the word of God speak to us. I was able to explain about the Adamic, Noahic, Abrahamic and New Covenants and show how our security is guaranteed because of the unconditionality of the promises of God. John, a new Christian from the university, told me how helpful the new understanding had been to him. We then got into an interesting discussion on predestination – I know it was a bit off the subject, but Terry had a question and that's the point of meeting in groups, isn't it? So as we didn't have time for group intercession, I closed the meeting with prayer, but I think I covered everything that was of concern to the group members.'

From one of the members:

'We had a wonderful time in our group last night. I could open up about my sister's illness and we were able to pray for healing. Joan said that she had real faith my sister would be healed. I was crying – some of the group hugged me. There is a real sense of togetherness here – not like church on Sunday. I feel really close to Jesus when I'm in the group. We chose some of our favourite songs – it was a lovely time of worship – a taste of heaven. The Bible study was very appropriate too – John 10 about the Good Shepherd. I was able to share how Jesus had been the perfect shepherd to me when I was so worried about my sister, especially when I attended the Life and Power Convention back in the Summer.'

When you meet as a group you will want to spend time praising God together, sharing your joys and sorrows and praying for one another. We will concentrate here on the group Bible study. The other aspects are covered in Units 4.6 and 4.7.

PREPARING THE BIBLE STUDY

Refer to UNIT 4.1 – *Using the Bible.*

Prepared material may be used but this is not a ready-made meal which you can serve up in 2½ minutes. The understanding, questions, discovery and vitality need to be your own.

UNDERSTANDING THE PASSAGE

 Let us take Matthew 12:1-14 as an example

Read the passage slowly twice and answer the following questions.

CONTEXT

1.Why does Matthew include this passage here?

2. How does it fit into the whole Gospel?

3. How does it fit into its immediate context?

4. What kind of literature is it?

CONTENT

1. What is the main theme or point?

2. What key words or themes are repeated?

3. Who are the main characters? How do they react to what is said and done?

4. What arguments does Matthew use?

5. When and where does this happen?

6. What do we learn about Christ?

7. What other Scriptures are referred to?

8. Is anything unclear to me?

Do your own reflection first. Then consult commentaries, dictionaries and any other sources.

CONSEQUENCES

Out of every Scripture there are consequences for both belief and behaviour. These are really two sides of the same coin. There may be direct promises to take to heart, and commands or warnings to heed but often the consequences will flow from what we learn of God and his dealings with the human race. The consequences may be personal or communal – for the church or for the world.

- **Communal** – how does this passage address our relationships in the group?
- **Personal** – what attitudes, beliefs, habits and values are addressed by the passage?
- **World** – how does this passage address our culture – its values and its treatment of people and things?

THAT'S A GOOD QUESTION

Context – You will probably have to supply most of the context, not to impress your group, but to put them in the picture. You will want to ask Content Questions (observation) and Consequence Questions (application).

What's wrong with the following questions? In answering, identify the pitfalls which can be encountered when devising questions.

- *Why did Jesus' disciples pick and eat the grain?*
- *What was the consecrated bread?*

- *Do you live as though the Son of Man is Lord of the Sabbath and not go to Sainsbury's on Sunday?*
- *What does this passage say about animal rights?*
- *Did Jesus mean that he was greater than the temple?*
- *What can we learn from these verses?*
- *Do you think the Pharisees were deliberately spying on Jesus?*
- *What was the Pharisees' hermeneutic of the Sabbath which gave rise to their disapproval of the actions of the disciples?*

1. Questions should always be stimulating, but what are the other characteristics of a good question?

2. Produce questions of your own.

LEADING THE BIBLE STUDY

The leader is not a lecturer. Preachers (especially aspiring ones) often make poor Bible study leaders. The set piece is much easier, as the whole agenda is within the preacher's control. But in a Bible study the leader's role is to raise the questions which the Bible raises – and having raised them to resist answering them! Direct the members of the group to Scripture so that they themselves may discover answers and perhaps raise questions of their own.

Read Luke 10:25-37

1. What can we learn from these verses about the way in which Jesus handled questions?

2. Think of a good small group Bible study leader you have known. What was it which made him or her so skilled and helpful? How did he or she handle:
- *over-talkative members?*
- *off-the-wall answers or side-tracks?*
- *controversial issues?*
- *personality clashes?*
- *silences?*

THINK IT THROUGH

How can your home group be used to reach others with the gospel? (Neighbourhood groups may have an advantage here). However, although mixing and matching your Christian and non-Christian friends is a good start, this alone won't bring people to Christ. So you will need a strategy.

FOLLOW IT UP

1. If your church has home groups, talk to your home group about giving themselves the following check-up:
- *Are people keen to come?*
- *Are newcomers welcome?*

- *Is there good overall participation – not just domination by the few?*
- *Are there any difficulties in relationships or communication?*
- *Are members learning from God's word?*
- *Is the Bible applied to their lives?*
- *Are members real and honest?*
- *Is there an enthusiasm to pray?*
- *Do members care for one another –practically as well as emotionally?*
- *Do members know one another well – for instance, are people aware of each other's work pressures, family concerns and spiritual passions?*
- *Are tasks shared between members?*
- *Are gifts being appropriately used?*
- *Is there evangelistic concern and initiative?*
- *Is the group supportive of the church and the church leaders?*
- *Are there windows to the world and to the global church?*
- *Does the group have a sense of purpose?*

2. If your church does not have home groups, how would you go about establishing them? Firstly, of course, you would have to raise the matter with the church leaders and gain a consensus in favour of the idea – we are not suggesting you begin an uprising.

LEADING GOD'S PEOPLE IN WORSHIP

'*THE PURPOSE OF GOD in sending his Son Jesus Christ to die and rise and live and be at the right hand of God the Father was that he might restore to us the missing jewel, the jewel of worship; that we might come back and learn to do again that which we were created to do in the first place – worship the Lord in the beauty of holiness, to spend our time in awesome wonder and adoration of God, feeling and expressing it, and letting it get into our labours and doing nothing except as an act of worship to Almighty God through his Son Jesus Christ.*' A.W. Tozer, Worship: The Missing Jewel of the Evangelical Church.

GET INTO THE BIBLE

When you hear the word 'worship' what do you think of?

Attempt a biblical definition of worship. Using a concordance will help, but the task of defining worship is complicated by the way in which different languages use different words. For example, all of the following Hebrew/Greek words could legitimately be translated as worship
- **avad** *(to serve) Exodus 4:23*
- **shahah** *(to bow) Psalm 95:6*
- **proskuneo** *(to adore, bow before) Matthew 14:33*
- **latreia/latreuo** *(ministry, to serve) Romans 12:1, Philippians 3:3*
- **leitourgeo** *(to perform priestly worship) Romans 15:15-16.*

Although we come to church to worship God, we also leave church to worship God! We see then two spheres of worship:

a. on active service – worship in the world

b. in assembled session – worship with the church

In this unit we are focusing on b. God has always called his people to come together out of the world to worship him. Our great destiny is to join the throng around the throne of God and the Lamb in incessant, exuberant worship (Revelation 4:9-11).

THE PATTERN OF WORSHIP

1. What does the order of service for corporate worship in your church look like?

For example, in a typical non-conformist church, this was at one time the standard form:

- *Scripture sentence*   *Minister*
- *Prayer (optional)*   *Minister*
- *Opening hymn*   *Minister*
- *Children's talk*   *Minister*
- *Children's hymn*   *Minister*
- *Offering/notices*   *Secretary*
- *Scripture reading*   *Minister*
- *Public prayer*   *Minister*
- *Hymn*   *Minister*
- *Sermon*   *Minister*
- *Closing hymn*   *Minister*
- *Blessing*   *Minister*

2. What are the strengths and weaknesses of the above order of service?

3. Is there a blueprint for corporate worship in the Bible? Is there a difference between the Old Testament and the New Testament?

'Whereas congregations today too often gather in a spirit of unexpecting apathy, scarcely aware that they come to church to receive, let alone to give, these Corinthians met with eagerness, excitement and expectation, anxious to share with their fellow believers the 'manifestation of the Spirit' that was theirs (1 Corinthians 12:7). Paul says, 'When you come together, everyone has a hymn, or a word of instruction, a revelation, a tongue or an interpretation.' (1 Corinthians 14:26). Public worship at Corinth was thus the very opposite of a drab routine. Every service was an event, for every worshipper came ready and anxious to share something God had given him. Paul gave regulations, not for creating this state of affairs, but for handling it in a way that was orderly and edifying once it had arisen. The state of affairs was itself the spontaneous creation of the Holy Spirit in that church. And when the Corinthians met for worship, the presence and power of God in their midst was an experienced reality.' **J I Packer, Serving the People of God, pp10–11**

What do you think of the above quotation? How would it be viewed and received in your church?

THE DYNAMICS OF WORSHIP

In the Old Testament, worship was prescribed and predictable. Everything had to be done in the right way by the right people. In the New Testament, there is much more freedom of form. Why do you think this is the case? Here are two reasons:
- Christ's sacrifice was exactly right and opened up a new way into God's presence (Hebrews 10:20)
- one of the reasons for the coming of the Holy Spirit was so that we may have liberty in our worship (2 Corinthians 3:12-18).

Whatever the freedom, the dynamics must be right.

Read the following verses:
Matthew 15:8, John 4:23-24, Psalm 24:3-4, Revelation 5:6-14

1. What do these verses teach us about worship?
2. It is common today to assume that we enter the presence of God through our worship.
- *Why is this assumption dangerous?*
- *How do we in reality enter the presence of God?*
- *When we grasp this, how will it affect our worship?*

THE BENEFITS OF CORPORATE WORSHIP

Look at the diagram on page 39. When we come together to worship God there is a two-way movement between 'the heavenlies' and earth. Grace comes down from God in Christ and his church acts as a prism directing the word of God onto and into our lives. Praise goes up from the people to

God, Father, Son and Spirit, the assembled church coming together as an orchestra to unite, harmonise and amplify praise.

Read Colossians 3:16

Looking at this model, what are the benefits of coming together in the name of Jesus to worship God?

GOD
CHRIST

Grace
...the word of his grace which can build you up...
Acts 20:32

Praise
...a sacrifice of praise – the fruit of lips that confess his name. Hebrews 13:15

CHURCH

Ministry gifts
Let the word of God dwell in you richly as you teach and admonish one another with all wisdom...Col 3:16a

Acts of devotion
...and as you sing psalms, hymns and spiritual songs in your hearts with gratitude in your hearts to God.. Col 3:16b

GOD'S
CHILDREN

THE ELEMENTS OF CORPORATE WORSHIP

Read the following passages:
- *Acts 2:42; 13:2*
- *Acts 4:34-37*
- *Acts 20:7-8*
- *1 Corinthians 14:26-31*
- *1 Corinthians 11:17-26*
- *Colossians 3:16*
- *Colossians 4:16*
- *Hebrews 10:25*

'Don't give up meeting together', exhorts the writer to the Hebrews. What did the church do when they met together?

Other elements from the Psalms involve:
- **Silence** – Psalm 46:10
- **Testimony** – Psalm 66:16
- **Expressions of rejoicing** – Psalm 149:1-3

LEADING CORPORATE WORSHIP

 What are the advantages and disadvantages of an open form of worship?

 Paul gives some principles in 1 Corinthians 14:26-32

As leader there will be a number of things you need to think and pray about if the service is to go well, both in connection with your preparation and your directing of the worship itself.

 Complete the table below by adding do's and don'ts of your own.

The Leader's – Do's and Don'ts	
Do's	**Don'ts**
Before the service	
Ask the question 'will the worship help people to' • prepare for the word? • respond to the word?	Use graphics which look as though they have come from local opticians where they were used as eyesight tests!
During the service	
Be real	Try to be funny or erudite, or try to show off your spiritual experiences. (People have come to worship God, not to notice you)

The Leader's – Do's and Don'ts	
Do's	**Don'ts**
After the service	
Seek some feedback	Fall into a fit of depression

THINK IT THROUGH

Prepare a service in which the sermon is from Romans 8:18-28 – The Triumph of Hope Over Experience. There are tensions in the Middle East and floods in Bangladesh. John and Linda had a minor accident on their way back from a very successful church workers' conference in Taxonia where they heard of many baptisms. Fred, who is 86, is seriously ill in the local hospital with heart failure. He and his wife, Alice, 82, are long-standing members of the church. One of their children (Margaret) is in the church – the other (Sheila) is not a believer. Amy, aged five, has very severe asthma and is in hospital. Her mum and dad, Tim and Emma, have another young child.

FOLLOW IT UP

Review last Sunday's morning or evening service. What did you appreciate? Was this a question of taste or theology? What did you not appreciate?

LEADING GOD'S PEOPLE IN PRAYER

'THE SUNDAY MORNING attendance shows how popular the church is. The Sunday evening attendance shows how popular the preacher is. The prayer meeting attendance shows how popular God is.'

Do you enjoy prayer meetings? What is the best prayer meeting you can remember? What made it special?

GET INTO THE BIBLE

The early church knew the value of meeting to pray. Well might C.H. Spurgeon encourage his own Monday night prayer meeting in Victorian London: 'Pentecost began with only a prayer meeting but ended with the grand baptism of thousands.'

Look at Acts 1:4-5,8

 What were they waiting for?

Read Acts 4:23-31

 1. What prompted this concerted prayer?
2. What is the starting point of this prayer? How does it develop? How do they pray?
3. What are the effects of this prayer?

Read Acts 12:1-17

As the chapter opens, Herod is rampant, Peter is behind bars and the church is on the defensive. By the end of it, Herod is dead, Peter is free and the word of God is on the march.

 What turns the tide in verse 5?

 When the church heard the knock at the door in the early hours they probably thought it was the secret police. How is this an encouragement to us? What makes these three prayer meetings different from many of ours?

Read the following verses:
• *Matthew 18:18-20*
• *Proverbs 27:17*
• *Ecclesiastes 4:12*
• *Joel 2:15-17*
• *Zechariah 8:21*

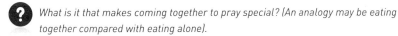 *What is it that makes coming together to pray special? (An analogy may be eating together compared with eating alone).*

A whole church on its knees is irresistible!

PREPARING (OR PRE-PRAYING) TO LEAD

A week in advance – ask yourself whether there are any special prayer burdens or priority areas. Announce this in the church newssheet or through the notices. Identify and ask those you wish to share in leading the meeting. Brief them clearly (time allowance; how their contribution will fit in with the purpose of the prayer meeting). At this stage you should be able to define the purpose of the prayer meeting.

DRAW NEAR TO GOD

At the start you will want to direct everyone's attention to God – especially his willingness and ability to answer prayer. We need to remember that we are speaking to God, how we approach him (through Christ), and to claim his promises. You may also like to praise him in song. The whole time needs to remain God-centred.

 'Be still and know that I am God.' How can we help folk to do this on a Thursday evening after a demanding day? What Scriptures can we use to encourage us to come before God?

CONFESS

This is never easy – especially in a group – but if it is neglected your prayer time may never get off the ground.

 See Luke 18:9-14, Isaiah 59:1-2, Daniel 9:20-22, James 1:6, 4:3

PRAY

Then you will want to pray!

 Read the following verses:
- *Luke 10:2*
- *Ephesians 6:18 (and see Paul's model prayers at the opening of some of his letters)*
- *Ephesians 6:19*
- *Colossians 4:3-4*
- *1 Timothy 2:2*
- *1 Timothy 2:4*

 For whom or what should we pray? You should keep some balance.

Practically:
- What further help or information will you need?
- Do you need to telephone anyone?
- Have you booked a suitable room?
- What visual presentation material or equipment will you need? (DVD,

PowerPoint, whiteboard or handouts)
- Will you need musicians, music or words?
- Looking back over past prayer meetings, what answers have you received?
- On the day – Arrive a little early. Check that the contributors are present, the room ready and the equipment in place.

THE PRAYER TIME

Round up all the prayer concerns and forthcoming ministry opportunities of the church. You will not be able to cover them all! Can you see a pattern emerging? Arrange the items into two, three or four sections.

The prayer meeting should be akin to the Israelites on their way to the promised land. They advanced in step with the pillar of cloud (daytime) or fire (nighttime) but lingered until it was time to move. When we have the sense of having discharged a prayer burden we too can move on.

There are many ways to pray. What are some of the advantages or disadvantages of:
- *solo praying in a united meeting?*
- *silent praying in a united meeting? – Bidding prayers are a cross between the two – the leader says: 'Let us pray for... our colleagues; those we meet in our everyday business; those who are now taking exams; our neighbours without Christ...' followed by silence.*
- *set praying in a united meeting? – the prayers are read.*
- *praying in pairs?*
- *praying in small groups?*
- *sentence praying? – everyone's limit is one sentence on a theme.*
- *chain praying? – round the room in a sequence.*
- *mobile praying? – moving round the room individually or in groups to locations where prayer information is displayed.*

There are two equal and opposite dangers of praying in public. One is to be oblivious of your fellow-pray-ers – the other is to be over-conscious of them. We need sensitivity to our Father in heaven and to our brothers and sisters in the room.

DEALING WITH PROBLEMS

1. What can spoil a prayer meeting? Two examples are the gossip shop and the long silence, but what others are there?
2. How would you deal with the following:
- ***Peacock pray-ers –*** *These are pray-ers who draw attention to 'me' – my feelings, my faith, my fortunes. All these prayers are usually prayed in the first person singular.*
- ***Drone pray-ers –*** *One night when George Whitefield was worn out from preaching*

that day he asked his host to pray before retiring. The man did so at such length that Whitefield rose from his knees while the prayer was still going on and groaned, 'Brother, how can you indulge in such tediousness? You prayed me into a delightful frame of mind, and you prayed me completely out of it again!'

• **Waspish pray-ers** – These pray-ers are those which set out to put other people right. Any lesser mortals who pray about ordinary, down-to-earth matters in plain English will certainly be intimidated by these self-consciously 'spiritual' men and women who use only the approved expressions of one of the superior brands of the Christian faith. Sometimes they mount a take-over bid. In his autobiography, one such 'wasp', Augustus Carp Esq, wrote: ' [I never allowed] an instant to elapse after the right to supplication had been declared general. Indeed, on many occasions I filled the subsequent gaps also, and at one particularly reluctant gathering, I can well remember offering a dozen full-length petitions in less than half-an-hour. That I soon had rivals goes without saying... But once started, I allowed no second petitioner to deflect or abbreviate my entreaties.'

• **Grasshopper pray-ers** – These pray-ers jump all over the shop and make no connection with anything prayed before. Just when the meeting is rising to the praise of the holiness of God, the grasshopper will suddenly break in with some sentiment such as 'God bless Mrs B with her septic toe.'

• **Cobweb pray-ers** – These pray-ers were very fresh once, but now their prayers are tired and gathering dust. The story is told of a dear old saint who would pray faithfully at every prayer meeting, 'Lord, sweep the cobwebs from our hearts; Lord, sweep the cobwebs from our hearts.' At one meeting when, true to form, he had made this petition 'Lord, sweep the cobwebs from our hearts,' one of the younger brothers could stand it no longer, and rising to his feet said in a loud voice – 'Lord, kill that spider!'

• **Whispering grass pray-ers** – These people always know the intimate details of the personal lives and problems of church members, and like to show they know.

• **Mouse pray-ers** – These may be a little shy, and thus need to be encouraged, or they may use hushed tones in prayer because of the solemnity of the occasion.

• **Wallflower pray-ers** – Those who stay silent do present a problem, as they are depriving both themselves and others of a real blessing.

• **Latebird pray-ers** – last but not least! A Christian Union leader at college once remarked, 'It's a good thing the CU is not a train – because if it were half of you would have missed it!'

FOLLOW IT UP

1. Ask your tutor for an opportunity to lead a prayer meeting. Ask a friend or your tutor to give feedback – what worked well, what didn't. (Remember the success of a prayer meeting depends only in part upon the leader. The Holy Spirit is the inspirer of our praying and God's people need to be open to him.)

2. How is your praying together as a church or leadership ministry team? If it is flagging at present, what can be done to give an injection of new life?

PLANNING AND PREPARING

THE AIM of these Units is to enable you to assess the need for, and develop, an evangelistic strategy which will enable your church to fulfil its God-given purpose of proclaiming the gospel.

To get you thinking, try these questions:

1. How would you define successful evangelism?

2. How would you differentiate evangelism from conversion?

3. Turn your mind to a yacht club and a lifeboat station.

• *What do these two institutions share in common?*

• *In what ways are they different?*

• *How do your answers apply to the church?*

GET INTO THE BIBLE

Read Acts 1:1-8

How would you describe Jesus' evangelistic strategy?

1. In the light of this, how would you define your 'Jerusalem'? And your 'Samaria'?

2. What kind of church is able to implement the Lord's strategy?

Read Acts 11:19-26

1. What was the impetus behind the evangelistic push described in these verses? Why might this be surprising?

2. What do some of the men from Cyprus and Cyrene do that is different?

3. How would you describe the planting of the church in Antioch?

The Holy Spirit led the early Christians to the main task of bringing people to Christ. Today, evangelism all too easily becomes a project in which we engage from time to time rather than a lifestyle that we live all the time.

Think about your own church.

1. How much money do you allocate each year for evangelism?

2. Which of the ministries of your church are evangelistic in focus?

3. For how many people in the church family is evangelism their main ministry?

4. What do your answers tell you about the priorities of your church?

WHAT IS HAPPENING NOW?

It is very important not to waste time reinventing the wheel, evangelistically. Talk to those in any form of leadership in your church. And talk to those in the church you know are keen on evangelism.

In the group, draw up a short questionnaire for the leaders of each activity in your fellowship (ladies meeting, youth group, etc) which will help them to evaluate the evangelistic quality of their ministry.

It is important to go back no further than about five years. The cultural differences between now and the days when 'all you had to do was put up a mission tent on the village green' are enormous and there is little strategic value in nostalgia.

THINK IT THROUGH

1. Why are church groups often ineffective in reaching unbelievers?
2. What holds churches back from being witnessing communities?
3. What could be done to make church groups more outward-looking?
4. At this point – before you carry out the questionnaire exercise – consider what you would do differently if you were starting a church from scratch.

FOLLOW IT UP

1. Using the questionnaire you have just prepared, survey the existing activities of the church.
2. Come prepared to discuss ways of developing the evangelistic focus of your church.

DEVELOPING A STRATEGY

A 'PEANUTS' CARTOON captures the evangelistic strategy of many churches. Charlie Brown is practising archery in his backyard. Instead of aiming at a target, he shoots at the fence and then walks over and draws a target around wherever the arrow strikes. Lucy walks up and says, 'Why are you doing this, Charlie Brown?' He replies, without embarrassment, 'This way I never miss!' A lot of evangelistic efforts in churches are hindered because there is no clear strategy behind them. Someone has an idea for a mission and lots of events are planned, but the 'bigger picture' is neglected. As a result effectiveness is reduced.

Read the following passages about Paul's ministry:

- *Acts 13:13-14, 49*
- *Romans 15:20-24*
- *Acts 17:1-4*
- *Acts 16:6-10*
- *1 Corinthians 9:19-23*
- *Acts 14:21-28*

What elements make up Paul's missionary strategy?

OUR STRATEGY

The first question which needs to be asked may seem a strange one – who are we trying to reach? The answer seems obvious – non-Christians. But which non-Christians? The problem is that non-Christians are not a uniform lot. There are many different sub-cultures.

Within the big picture, Paul is careful, recognising cultural distinctives and addressing each group accordingly.

Read Acts 17:16-31

1. Before Paul launches into his gospel ministry in Athens, what does he do?

2. How does this shape his evangelistic approach?

3. In what ways does he show his understanding of Greek culture?

4. Which 'poets' do we need to be familiar with today?

Decide whether your evangelism will have geographical boundaries or sociological ones. Will you evangelise everyone in a given area (usually the area around the church)? Or will you target a particular group? This group may not be based around the church but may include people from much further afield, such as the work colleagues of the members of your church.

Many churches are utterly unrealistic where this is concerned and without thinking about the consequences simply opt for the geographical boundary because it is easier.

1. What are the geographical boundaries of your church?

2. What different people-groups are contained within it?

Some churches talk about people-group evangelism, among groups like schoolteachers or mums and tots.

It is vital to understand that evangelism cannot be separated from the church to which you are inviting people to hear the gospel. When, how and if you invite people to church will depend a lot on where the church is in terms of its openness to outsiders coming in.

Read the scenario described below. It is intended to be a fictitious story but may be relevant to quite a number of current churches.

Wigton Street Evangelical Church was in the middle of a 1960s housing estate. At one time it had been full every Sunday and had a thriving youth work. Now the estate was very run down. There was a large socially-excluded white population and an increasing representation from ethnic minorities. However the church membership all travelled in from the nicer suburban areas. Only Mr and Mrs Smith still lived on the estate. The church was almost all white. The worship was very traditional. Since the Sunday school was held separately in the afternoon, any children who came in the morning sat through the entire sermon. The church had tried to evangelise. A few years ago, the 'Is this the Way to Life?' team came with their big tent. Door-to-door had been done. Some people had come to the services, but didn't stay. 'No commitment nowadays!' was the Pastor's comment.

1. The geographical boundary is clear in the above scenario, but there is a sociological barrier too. List as many aspects of that barrier as you can think of.

2. How can a church in this situation begin to overcome these sociological differences?

3. Why might some members be reluctant to do any of this?

4. Imagine you are a young person in your 20s with absolutely no Christian background attending this church for the first time. Think about how you would feel. How much do you think you would understand?

5. How different from the above scenario (be honest!) is your own church?

If you feel that it may not be best to take your friend to church straight away, a good alternative could be to offer a home Bible study. Instead of expecting the unbeliever to come to you, go to them and hold a weekly or fortnightly study in their home. Your church leaders will point you to the wide range of evangelistic material that is available. The advantage of this approach is that the gospel can be explained to your friend in what they consider a safe environment. It also gives time for a relationship to be built before they finally come along to the church. That way they will feel they know someone when they do come along.

Method	Advantages	Disadvantages	Target Group	Cost (high, medium or low)
Door-to-door				
Open air preaching				
Christianity Explored-type course				
Team quiz night at the church				
Family Sunday in local park				
Evangelistic meal				
Evangelistic services				
Tract distribution				

METHOD

Time needs to be given to considering what forms of outreach you will use. There are all the obvious ones: door-to-door, evangelistic services, Christianity Explored-type courses. It may be that you can think of something that would be especially appropriate for the area or people-group you are trying to reach.

Look at the methods in the chart above and consider the advantages and disadvantages, the target audience and the cost of each activity to those involved. By cost, we mean finance, energy, time, emotion and relationships with friends and neighbours. Add any other methods which you can suggest.

The approach you use will to some degree be dictated by the resources (people and money) available to you. It may be worth asking your church leadership for a specific budget which you could use to buy materials, book venues or to meet other costs. It is better to do a few things well than to over-stretch yourselves and to do something on a larger scale which is of poor quality.

THINK IT THROUGH

1. Which people-groups could be reached by church-based evangelism in your area?
2. What support will be required to implement an evangelistic strategy in your church?

FOLLOW IT UP

Create an evangelistic diary for the next year based on the principles described in this Unit.

IMPLEMENTING THE STRATEGY

THE AIM of this Unit is to look at the practicalities of leading evangelism and implementing an evangelistic strategy. We will look at five areas of running an evangelistic team in your church, including prayer, training, motivation, managing expectations and follow-up.

PRAYER

 Read Colossians 4:2-6

 1. For whom does Paul seek prayer? And why?
2. For what specific things does Paul pray?
3. What is the difference between Paul's ministry and the ministry of the Colossian Christians?

Ultimately it is the Lord who saves and prayer is crucial to seeing God's purposes fulfilled on earth.

 1. Looking back to Paul's instructions, what should you be praying for?
2. How can you encourage the church to pray for evangelism?
3. How can you ensure that people are kept up to date with prayer needs?
4. How can you ensure that people who are praying feel part of the evangelistic team?

TRAINING

Read the passages in the diagram and link them with the appropriate training methods.

Matthew 5-7	Having a go
Matthew 8-9	Reporting back
Matthew10:1-16	Teaching
Mark 6:30-31 (parallel to the Matthew passages)	Modelling

Fill in the box below

Training Method	What knowledge/skills do you want to include?	How will you do this?
Teaching		
Modelling		
Having a go		
Reporting back		

MOTIVATION

It is one thing to put together an evangelistic outreach for a short period of time, but it is quite another to have a team who will sustain that work over months and years. In the present spiritual and cultural climate only long-term evangelism will be really fruitful. That means that it will need a particular kind and quality of input and guidance if the outreach effort is not to die away as enthusiasm wanes.

1. List some of the reasons why enthusiasm wanes.
2. What can be done about it?

One of the main reasons which you may have identified is lack of results. The team don't see anyone come to faith in the first few months and so are discouraged and think about doing something else in the church. This discouragement arises from two sources:
   • wrong expectations and
   • inadequate follow-up.

MANAGING EXPECTATIONS

Whenever evangelism is planned Christians begin, quite rightly, to pray for people to be saved. Unless they are clearly given some guidance on this, however, many will think it is going to happen in the first few weeks. This is largely a legacy from the days when Britain was a Christianised country and many people knew the gospel, even though they hadn't yet responded to it. Evangelism was giving them the opportunity to respond.

That is not the situation today. Many people have no idea what the gospel is about, so how can they be expected to respond as the result of one visit, or reading a leaflet, or attending a gospel service?

The team needs to understand that evangelism today is a process. Non-Christians have to start from scratch putting all the pieces together about who God is, why we need to be forgiven and many other truths. It is important therefore for the church to have high, faith-filled, but realistic expectations.

FOLLOW-UP

A crucial part of maintaining morale is for the follow-up to be effective so that the team can see the work progressing. People can cope with no immediate converts if they can see that there are people moving towards a position of faith. This is a crucial area which so many churches get wrong, resulting in discouraged church members and confused unbelievers.

It is essential with follow-up to realise that people will broadly fall into one of three categories:
- those who reject the gospel outright. They may change their mind at some point in the future but, for the present, they can be left alone.
- those in whom the Lord is already at work and who make some sort of immediate response, such as coming to church or starting a study.
- those who do not reject the gospel. They are quite interested, but they are not yet at the stage where they are going to go to a church service or start a Bible study. They are in a no-man's land. What they need is for the link to be maintained until the Lord begins to move them towards faith in Christ —often as the result of a relationship of trust developing with those who are Christians already.

1. Discuss ways in which non-intrusive contact can be maintained with those in this last group. Some are obvious like delivering a monthly church newsletter. How many other ways can you identify?
2. How can a visitor from the church facilitate the building of this contact?
3. What might ruin it?

The team will also remain motivated if they feel that they are appreciated within the church. Obviously no-one should be motivated by a desire for personal glory or status, but some recognition by the church leadership of what they are doing and of some of the struggles they are facing can go a long way towards maintaining encouragement.

DEVELOPING THE WORK

It is important to be flexible as the evangelism develops. There can be no room for maintaining something out of tradition or habit. Every form of outreach needs to be reviewed regularly and altered as required. Encourage the team to suggest different forms of evangelism. While there is little point in slavishly following trends, it is important to be aware of other people's ideas for evangelism and to try any that seem worthwhile.

It is especially important to encourage new converts to have input into the team.

One of the most important aspects of maintaining the team will be your input and example as leader and organiser. If you can stay excited about the task, then that will have an encouraging effect on the rest. This means that the quality of your own spiritual life is of the utmost importance.

The team needs to pray together on a regular basis and to begin to get to know each other. Some churches allow the evangelism team to become a house group so that they can do this.

Discuss the strengths and weaknesses of this approach

THINK IT THROUGH

1. What evangelistic methods are working in other churches near you? How might your evangelistic team assess the merits of these methods for adoption in your church?

2. It is especially important to encourage new converts to have input into the team. Discuss the pros and cons of involving new converts.

3. The team needs to pray together regularly and really begin to get to know each other. Some churches allow the evangelism team to become a home group so that they can do this. Discuss the strengths and weaknesses of this approach.

FOLLOW IT UP

If your church doesn't have an evangelism team, draw up proposals to create one...

1. Who might have the gifts, time and commitment to lead it?

2. What kind of people should be invited to join it?

3. What resources will it require?

4. What kind of support will be necessary to sustain it?

BE PREPARED
to serve the LORD

Prepared for Service **provides a unique, part-time training opportunity for both men and women with a desire to serve the Lord Jesus Christ and his people, to be better equipped for works of service in local churches, their communities and the world.**

It aims to achieve this by:

- Offering an environment where gifts and abilities can be realistically assessed to help understand God's purpose for an individual's life

- Providing a biblically-based training resource to help individuals develop knowledge of God's word within the framework of academic study

- Giving practical and pastoral models helping individuals serve in ways that are appropriate to the contemporary world

- Providing teaching, pastoral care and practical experience for individuals with the support of their local churches

For Information Pack/Application Form, please contact:

PREPARED FOR SERVICE

The 'PfS' Administrators
25, Felton Road,
Poole, Dorset. BH14 0QR

Tel: 01202 738416
Email: pfs@fiec.org.uk
Web: www.fiec.org.uk

FIEC
Bible churches together

A Training Ministry of
The Fellowship of Independent Evangelical Churches

Could PfS fulfil your needs in serving the LORD?

NOTES

Continue your studies at home with the
Open Bible Institute
— a thoroughly Bible-centred, distance-learning college

One of the great seats of learning

• **Short Courses in ministry skills:** 10-session courses in Administration, Christian Mission & Ministry, Pastoral Care, Preaching and Youth & Children's Work.

• **The Moore College Correspondence Course:** a great course encompassing biblical studies, church history, doctrine, apologetics and ethics.

• **Certificates of Higher Education:** fully validated qualifications in 'Biblical Studies and Theology' and 'Biblical Studies and Ministry' equivalent to the first year of a degree.

For an information pack or an informal
discussion, please contact:
0845 225 0885
admin@open-bible-institute.org
www.open-bible-institute.org

open bible institute

NOTES

Certification

If you would like your work to be assessed by an independent organisation then please send a clearly named folder containing answers to all the exercises in the this book to the Open Bible Institute:

The Open Bible Institute
Elm House
37 Elm Road
New Malden
Surrey KT3 3HB, UK

A marking fee is payable. For full details please see the website:
www.open-bible-institute.org/learn2lead

Authors

Learn2Lead was developed by:
Brian Boley
Richard Underwood
Paul Mallard
Dr Ray Evans
Tim Saunders